The Adventures of SUPER DiAPER BABY

Thats me!

THE FiRST EPiC NOVEL
BY George Beard and Harold Hutchins

SCHOLASTIC

For my mom and Dad — G.R.B.
To mom and Heidi — H.M.H.

Scholastic Children's Books
An imprint of Scholastic Ltd
Euston House, 24 Eversholt Street
London, NW1 1DB, UK
Registered office: Westfield Road, Southam, Warwickshire, CV47 0RA
SCHOLASTIC and associated logos are trademarks
and/or registered trademarks of Scholastic Inc.

First published in the US by Scholastic Inc, 2002
First published in the UK by Scholastic Ltd, 2002

This edition published 2014

Copyright © Dav Pilkey, 2002

The right of Dav Pilkey to be identified as the author
of this work has been asserted by him.

Trade ISBN 978 1407 14791 8
Non-trade ISBN 978 1407 15384 1

A CIP catalogue record for this book is available from the British Library.

Printed and bound in by CPI Group (UK) Ltd, Croydon, CR0 4YY
Papers used by Scholastic Children's Books are made from wood grown in sustainable forests.

1 3 5 7 9 10 8 6 4 2

This is a work of fiction. Names, characters, places, incidents and dialogues are products
of the author's imagination or are used fictitiously. Any resemblance to actual people,
living or dead, events or locales is entirely coincidental.

www.scholastic.co.uk

Be sure to check out
Dav Pilkey's Extra-Crunchy Web Site O' Fun at
www.pilkey.com

☆ The ORIGIN of ☆ SuPer DiaPer BaBy

A introduction by George Beard and Harold Hutchins

Once upon a time there were two cool kids named George and Harold.

were the Bomb!

me Too.

One time they were in the gym Running over ketchup packs on their Skatebords.

HA HA

HA HA

SPLASH SQUIRT

SQUIRT

It was Fun until their mean Principle, MR. Krupp came by.

HEY

CLEAN up this Mess!

When Your done Meet me in my OFFICE, bubs!

So they cleaned up the gym floor....

SSSSS

...And went to mr. Krupps office.

You Boys are very iresponsible.

Normally I'd would make you write sentences for a punishment..... but that doesnt teach you anything!

So instead I'm Going to make you write A 100 page essay on "Good Citizenship".

And I dont want you kids turning in a 100-page comic Book About "captain Underpants" either! Thats is UN-ACCE-ptible

Aw man

no Fair

George and Harold were Bummed.

Why can't we make a comic Book About captain Underpants?

Yeah—He's A good citizen!

Then They got a great idea!

Hey, Let's make up a new super Hero And write A comic About him!

O.K.

So they went home and got to work.

The next day they turned in their 100-Page "essay"

What the---

... AnD SO...

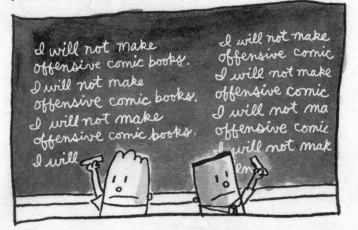

So thats the story of how Super Diaper Baby was invented.

We hope you Like it more than Mr. Krupp did.

Treehouse Comix Inc.

The Adventures of SUPER DiAPER BABY

By George Beard And Harold Hutchins

Chapters

The Advenchers of
★SUPER★
DiAPer BABY

CHAPTER 1
"A Hero is Born"

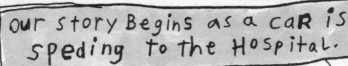

Our story Begins as a caR is speeding to the Hospital.

10

11

But what Mr. and Mrs. Hoskins Dident know was that there new Baby would have a Job...As A **Super Hero!**

Delivery Room

weee

But... Before We can tell you that Story, we Have to tell you **This story.**

This is Deputy Dangerous and Danger DOG. Deputy Dangerous is the one on The Left with the Cowboy Hat and the aposible thumbs. Danger Dog is the one on the right with the Tail and the Flea problem.

Remember That now.

EVIL PLANS

To secret LABratory

Deputy Dangerous was mean and Ruthless.

I'm am evil too

Danger Dog was also bad too.

I'm not really evil. I'm Just in it for The Kibbles.

Hey SHUT UP!

Together they opened up a Underware Laundry. But it was a TRAP!

YE Old Underware CLEANers

underware cleaned while you wait

super Heros Welcome

Soon came the moment that Deputy Dangerous was waiting for.

Tra-La-Laaaa!

YE Old Under CLEAN

Look whose Hear! Its Captain Underpants!

My Hero!

14

What HAPPEND? I- I- I Feel So weak.

Thats Because I took Your powers Away. Haw Haw Haw

Behold: Your super powers were Transformed into This Juice.

ALL we Have to do is drink This super power Juice And we will get super powers!

Cool!

You drink HalF Then I'LL drink HalF. Then we will RULE The world.

O.K.

GLUB GLUB Glub

KA·POW

15

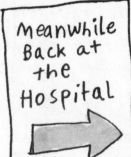

Meanwhile Back at the Hospital

PUSH!

POP

Congrajulashons! You got a Baby Boy.

Now I have to Give him the "spank of Life".

Aw man, cant you Just give him a time-out?

Hey You stupid Baby! You drank all my SUPER-POWER JUICE! —Give it to Me NOW!!!

Uh oh...

WARNING

THE Following pages contains scenes showing A baby beating up a ~~bad~~ bad guy.

Get ready to be OFFended......

Graphic violins

FLiP·O·RAMA

HERE's HOW it WORKS!!!!

STEP 1
PLase your LeFt Hand inside the dotted Lines marked "LeFt HAND Here." Hold the Book open FLAT.

STEP 2
GRasp The Right-hand Page with Your Right thumb and index Finger (inside the dotted Lines marked "Right THUMB Here").

STEP 3
Now Quickly Flip the Right-hand page back and FOURTH until the Pitcher appears to Be Animated!

(for extra fun, try adding your own Sound-AFecks)

23

FLIP-O-RAMA # 1

(Pages 25 and 27)

Remember, flip <u>only</u> Page 25. while you are fliping, be shure you can see the Pitcher on Page 25 <u>And</u> the one on Page 27.

IF you flip Quickly, the two pitchers will start to look like <u>one</u> Animated pitcher.

Don't forget to add your own Sound Affecks

Left Hand Here

take this!

right
Thumb
Here

take this!

FLIP·O·RAMA #2

(pages 29 and 31)

Remember, flip only page 29.
while you are fliping, be shure
you can see the pitcher on
page 29 And the one on
page 31.

If you flip quickly,
the two pitchers will
start to look like one
Animated pitcher.

Don't forget to
add your own
Sound Affecks

Left Hand
Here

... And that!

right
Thumb
Here

... And that !

FLIP-O-RAMA #3

(pages **33** and **35**.)

Remember, FLip only page 33. while you are Fliping, be shure you can see the pitcher on page 33 and ~~page~~ page 35.

IF you FLip Quickly, the two pitchers will start to Look like yadda yadda yadda.

Don't forget to skip these pages without reading them.

Left Hand Here

... And some of these!

right
Thumb
Here

...And some of these!

37

Ha-Ha. I hope Theres no hard feelings About my little spanking Acksident. Ha-ha.

HeY!

FLiP· ·O· RAMa #4

LeFt Hand Here

ALL is Forgiven

right
Thumb
Here

ALL is Forgiven

So Mr. and Mrs. Hoskins took there new Baby "Billy" home from the hospital.

SUPER DI-APER BABY

Chapter 2
"The Evil Plan"

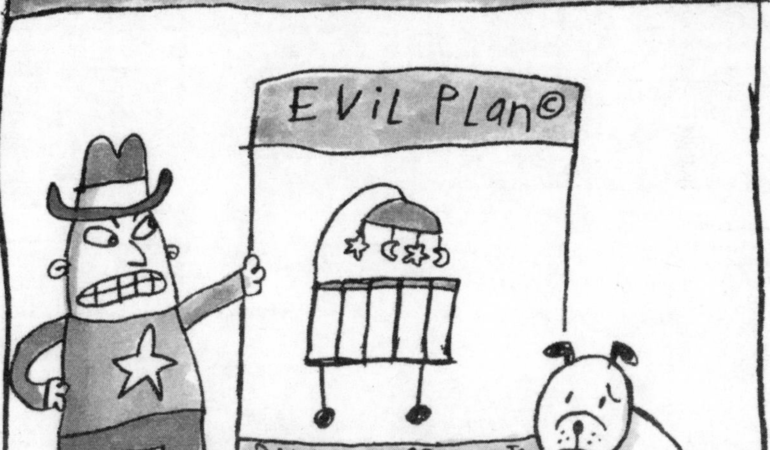

Deputy Dangerous and Danger Dog went straight to jail. But they exscaped.

Then they flew to a secret Labratory high on a mountain.

Now I will invent a invenchion to Get REVENGE!!!

So Deputy Dangerous worked all night on the Danger-CRIB 2000.™

44

45

46

that Night

Good night, Billy.

Sleep Good in your new crib.

Meanwhile Back at The secret Lab...

Transfer Helmet

Haw Haw Haw! It's almost midnight. Soon I will be Transformed!

B U T

At 11:59 PM, something unexpeckted Happened.

MOMMA!

47

48

But at that very moment the poop was being beamed to a satelite.

And soon it was beamed back to earth...

...Right to Deputy Dangerouses transfer helmet.

49

FLiP-O-RAMA 5

Left Hand Here

---Aw Maaaaan!!!

---Aw Maaaaan!!!

SUPER DIAPER *BABY*

CHAPTER 3
Dial "R" for "Revenge."

When they got back to there Labratory, Deputy Dangerous began making a all-new invention.

60

63

Your supposed to be destroying the world, bub!

I am, Deputy Doo-Doo.

No your not --- your just goofing off as usual!

And stop calling me that!

tee hee

Meanwhile at the Hoskinses House...

Mrs. Hoskins was washing dishes when she saw a horible sight.

65

ker-
KRAK

right
Thumb
Here

Who's Afraid of
the Big, Bad
Bug?

FLIP·O·RAMA #7

(pages **73** and **75.**)

Remember, flip **only** page 73.
while you are fliping, be
shure to blah, blah, blah.
You're not really reading
this page, are you?

well, since your here
anyway, how about a
gross joke? Q: What's
the difference between
boogers and broccoli?

A: kids
wont eat
broccoli.

LeFt Hand
Here

ALL Shook up!!!

right
Thumb
Here

ALL Shook up!!!

FLIP-O-RAMA #8

(pages **77** and **79**.)

Remember, Flip <u>only</u> page 77.
You know, since nobody
reads these pages, we figured
they'd be a good place to
insert subliminimal messages:

Think for yourself.
Question Authority. Read
banned books! Kids have
the same constitutional
rights as grown-ups!!!

Don't forget to
boycott standardized
testing!!!

Left Hand
Here

Watch out, BiLLy!!!

right
Thumb
Here

Watch out, BiLLy!!!

SUPER DiAPER BABY

★ ★ ★ ★ ★ ★

CHAPTER 4
" HOORAY FOR Diaper DOG "

So Danger Dog Flew Billy back to his parents house.

Hey Look, it's Safety Dog!

Hooray

DOGGY saved me!

WOW

How would you like to Live with us?

Hold it right There! I'm the Landlord and I don't allow no dogs!!!

How come?

Because he might go pee-pee on the carpet!!!

What if we make him wear a diaper?

Hmmm--- I guess that will be O.K.

And so Danger Dog changed his name to "Diaper Dog"...

Tee Hee

Doggy needs blankie.

Heres is a extra Blanket

... And a new crime fighting duo was born.

BUT....

Meanwhile at the New clear Power Plant, something terrible was Happening to Deputy Doo-Doo.

Dont call me that!

87

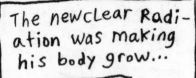

The newclear Radiation was making his body grow...

... and Grow...

... and grow...

... until suddenly...

I'm Gonna get You, Super Diaper Baby...
...and your Little DOG Too!

You know, I've seen People Step on Poo Before, but I've never seen Poo Step on people!

Yeah, life is funny that way.

88

meanwhile at the Hoskinses House...

I will get Desert

Look up in the sky... It's A Turd!

It's A Plane!

...No wait. You're Right... It's A turd.

KiBBLES

And so with Lightning speed, our heros Tied on their blankies.

And oFF they FLew.

"Poopy-Puncher"

right
Thumb
Here

"Poopy - Puncher"

FLiP-O-RAMA #10

Left Hand Here

Head Banger Blues

right
Thumb
Here

Head Banger
Blues

FLIP-O-
RAMA #11

Left Hand
Here

Around and Around
they went

right
Thumb
Here

Around and Around
they went

SUPER DIAPER BABY

CHAPTER 5
"HapiLy Ever After"

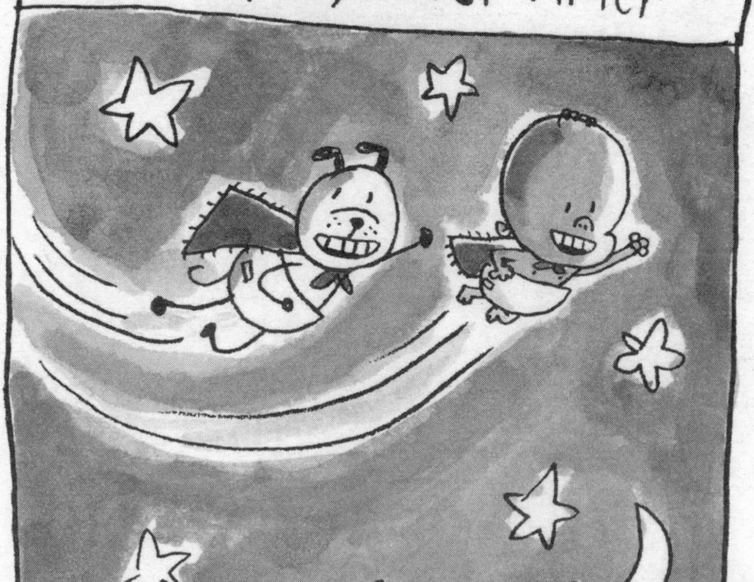

On there way back our Heros stopped at Mars for some refreshments.

Man, these places are everywhere!

Can I help you?

Yeah, I'll take a large water... and a juice box for the kid.

Me like juice box.

New Alien Super-Power Juice

Gives you super powers!

SUPER power juice

Will there be anything else, sir?

Hmmm

THE LAST FLIP-O-RAMA

Left Hand Here

And they all Lived
Hapily ever After

right
Thumb
Here

And they all Lived
Hapily ever After

HOW 2 DRAW
SUPER DIAPER BABY

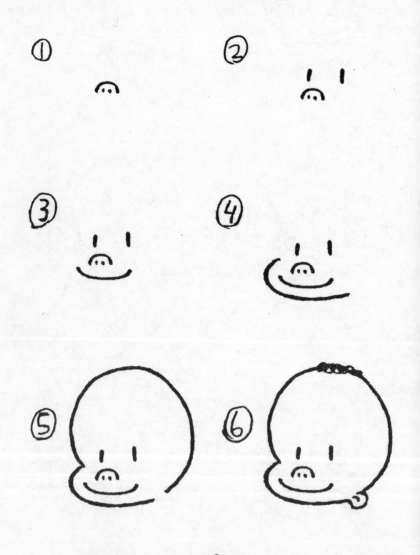

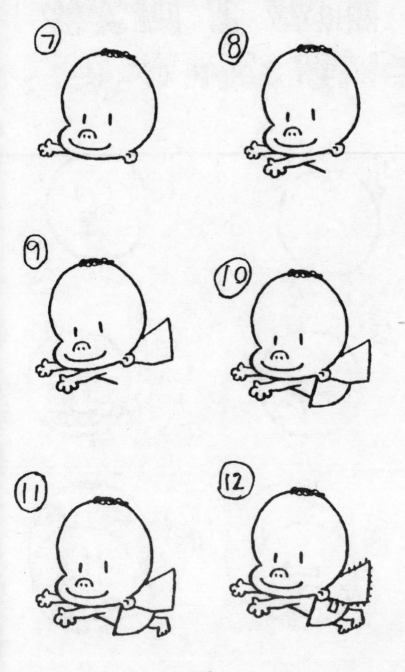

How 2 Draw
Diaper Dog

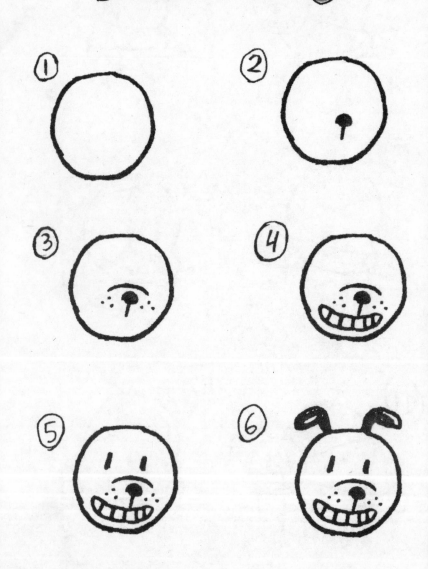

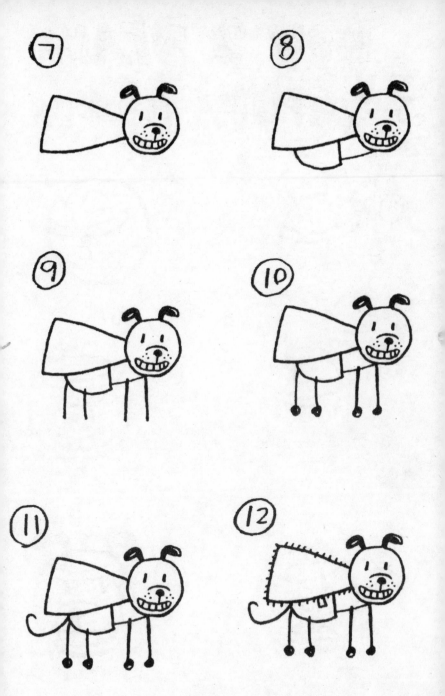

How 2 Draw Deputy Doo-Doo

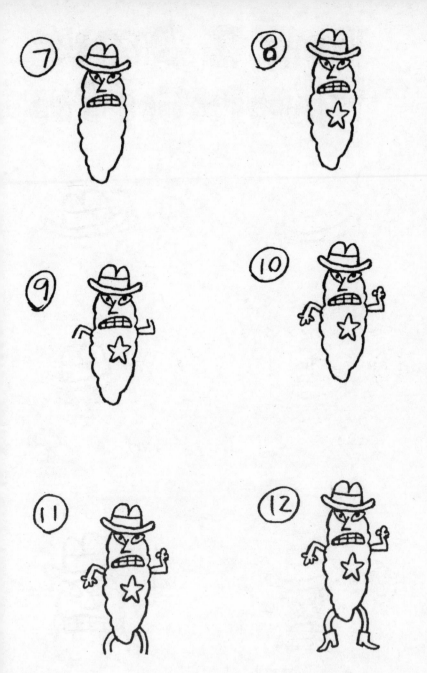

HOW 2 DRAW
The Robo-Ant 2000

124

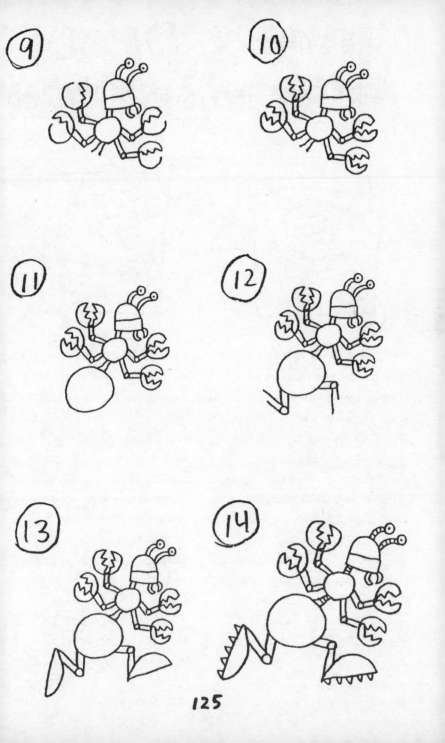

125

About the Author and Illustrator

GEORGE BEARD (age 9 ¾) is the co-creator of such wonderful comic book characters as Captain Underpants, Timmy the Talking Toilet, and The Amazing Cow Lady.

Besides making comics, George enjoys skateboarding, watching TV, playing video games, pulling pranks, and saving the world. His favorite food is chocolate chip cookies.

George lives with his mom and dad, and his two cats, Porky and Buckwheat. He is currently a fourth grader at Jerome Horwitz Elementary School in Piqua, Ohio.

HAROLD HUTCHINS (age 10) has co-written and illustrated more than 30 comic books with his best pal (and next-door neighbor), George Beard.

When he is not making comics, Harold can usually be found drawing or reading comics. He also enjoys skateboarding, playing video games, and watching Japanese monster movies. His favorite food is gum.

Harold lives with his mom and his little sister, Heidi. He has five goldfish named Moe, Larry, Curly, Dr. Howard, and "Superfang."

We're Sorry !!!

If you were offended by this book, please send your name and address on a postcard to:

Your name
and Address

"Me was offended by
Super Diaper Baby"
The publicity Department
Scholastic Children's Books
Euston House
24 Eversholt Street
London NW1 1DB

... and we'll send you more offensive stuff!

The Adventures of SUPER DIAPER BABY

Behind the Baby

Read on for the behind-the-scenes story about the making of this book, pages from Dav Pilkey's sketchbook, and more!

THE STORY BEHIND THE STORY

In case you didn't know, this book was really written by George and Harold's alter ego — me! My name is Dav Pilkey. That's me on the right.

George and Harold are very real characters to me. I based both of them on myself when I was a kid. So when I started working on this book, I needed to "become" George and Harold. In my imagination, I stopped being me, and sort of let them take over. I let them create the story they wanted, without worrying about spelling, or grammar, or moralistic plots that would please adults.

I was also inspired by the homemade comic books I receive from kids every day. Their comics sometimes contain poor grammar and misspelled words, and usually have bad guys who are disgusting in one way or another.

But the amazing thing is that these comics are all made voluntarily. Nobody forces those kids to make comic books. They just do it for fun. And there's always something wonderful about that kind of unprompted creativity. I really tried to capture some of that energy in this book.

Part 1: THE INSPIRATION

When I was making *Captain Underpants and the Wrath of the Wicked Wedgie Woman* (which contains three comics by George and Harold), I began to imagine how much fun it would be to do an entire book of comics.

At first, I wanted to do a collection of short, unrelated comic stories by George and Harold. I wrote down a bunch of ideas and titles. But Super Diaper Baby didn't really appear until I began

to draw sketches. This sketch was the beginning of everything. I liked the way the baby looked so much that I immediately decided to do a whole book about him.

Part 2: THE SKETCHES

When I first begin to work out a story (which I usually do in my head), it helps me to have visual references. So I like to draw sketches of the main characters, and write down who they are and what role they will play in the story.

Here are my first character sketch sheets:

Danger Dog

Mom: Ellen Hoskins

Dad: Ralph Hoskins

Super Draper Baby

Billy Hoskins

Diaper DOG

Part 3: FIGURING OUT THE STORY

Usually, I find it helpful to make notes on a story BEFORE I write it. The next two pages are from an early draft.

You'll notice that these pages have pictures in the margins.

I find that it's helpful to draw while I write, because I often get good ideas from my sketches.

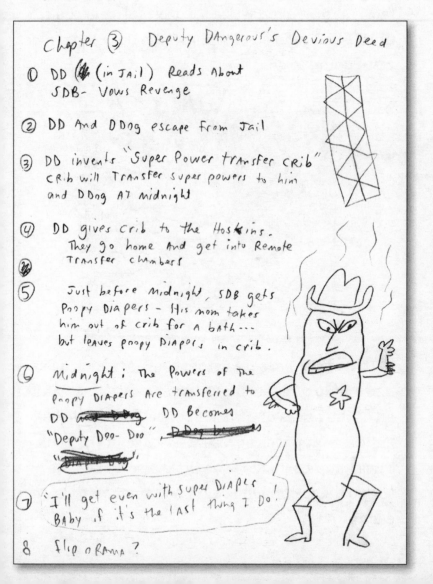

Chapter ③   Deputy DAngerous's Devious Deed

① DD ~~#~~ (in Jail) Reads About SDB— Vows Revenge

② DD And DDog escape from Jail

③ DD invents "Super Power transfer Crib" Crib will Transfer super powers to him and DDog AT midnight

④ DD gives crib to the Hoskins. They go home And get into Remote Transfer chambers

⑤ Just before midnight, SDB gets Poopy Diapers — His mom takes him out of crib for a bath... but leaves poopy Diapers in crib.

⑥ Midnight: The Powers of the Poopy Diapers Are transferred to DD ~~and DDog~~ DD Becomes "Deputy Doo-Doo", ~~DDog becomes~~ ~~"DiAper Dog"~~

⑦ "I'll get even with super DIApers BABy if it's the last thing I Do!"

⑧ flip oRama?

Part 4: THE STORYBOARDS

I created this book in a different way from
most of my other books because the story and
art were more important than the writing. In
fact, I didn't even write the text for this book
until I had figured out where the drawings
were going to go.

To do this, I created storyboards, which are
like a map of the book. They show an illustrator
all of the pages of a book at once.Each little box
on the next page represents a page in the book.
The sketches inside each little box helped me
to decide how much room I had to put words on
each page.

Part 5: THE DUMMY

After the storyboards were completed, I made a dummy, which is kind of like a rough draft. This is where I did most of the work on the book. If you look closely at the next group of pictures, you'll see that I was still trying to figure out parts of the story at this stage.

There are many differences between what appears in the dummy and what ended up in the book.

Part 6: THE EDITING

During the editing process, changes often need to be made. I decided to drop several panels from chapter 1 because I felt that they slowed down the pace of the story.

Part 7: THE COVER

Then it was time to draw the cover.

Here is a pencil sketch:

Finally, it was time to start painting!